The Taste of Glass

Clive Donovan

LEAF BY LEAF

Published by Leaf by Leaf
an imprint of Cinnamon Press
www.cinnamonpress.com

The right of Clive Donovan to be identified as author of this work has been asserted by him in accordance with the Copyright, Designs and Patent Act, 1988. © 2021, Clive Donovan.
ISBN 978-1-78864-927-8

British Library Cataloguing in Publication Data. A CIP record for this book can be obtained from the British Library.

Designed and typeset in Bodoni by Cinnamon Press.
Cover design by Adam Craig © Adam Craig.
Cinnamon Press is represented by Inpress

Acknowledgements

Some of these poems have been published in the following magazines. I am grateful to their editors:
Acumen, Algebra of Owls, Ariadne's Thread, Brittle Star, Cake, Cannons Mouth, Crannog, Dreamcatcher, Dreich, Erbacce, The High Window, Ink Sweat & Tears, The Journal, Orbis, Pennine Platform, Picaroon, Poetry Salzburg Review, Prole, Sarasvati, Sentinel Literary Quarterly, Seventh Quarry, Skylight 47, The Transnational, Two Thirds North.

Yes indeed, the world has turned grey
But it is a bright, bright grey

For Lucy and Celia

Contents

The Taste of Glass

The Frame

So, as with this frame I was sold walking homeward
figuring which poster would look good in wood,
I paused to watch the world unfold
as spectacles arose:
Selecting compositions,
abstracting dusty tableaux,
angling for scenes I scried as
busy histories or mysteries.

Then you come
To fill the frame;
Become a laughing picture –
famously familiar.
First you
        kiss
              the pane
Then
     reach over to
                 kiss me,
the still trapped portrait of a witness
on the other side.
Your lips taste of glass.

Misty Morning

On this autumn misty morning
should I take a mournful ramble,
pity-touched among the filled tombs,
examining engraved inscriptions,
swishing at pods in the uncut grass,
picking at body-fed berries in brambles?
or, could be, a visit to market,
there to prod at cabbages,
see what days remain in them,
or go and buy some persimmons?
I need a new pen, a light bulb, some string.

Perhaps I'll meet a somebody other
on a similar errand;
one person who knows the impossible miracle
of this alive, shared day;
of news, of coffee, signs in the sky,
of river-gazing, getting high,
watching moss grow, plotting larks,
or just plodding the pavements together,
sparks shooting from our shoes,
kicking them up for the glow.

It is Sufficient

It is sufficient to see the blush of promised dawn,
the deep blue sky ridden by cotton puffs of chariots

and not to see like fish or flies – faceted,
orbital, telescopic, magnified,

not coveting the thoughtless worm's felicity
nor placid trees, rooting slow, swelling their time-rings.

It is enough to stroll in simple grass, strip seeds, chuck them high,
be charmed by skylarks and curlews, not envying their song,

nor the rich, naked, natural lives of fox and hare,
who stop to stare, plain as stone, till I move on,

emergent into this bliss-trance of beauty manifest
for its own perfect sake – not mine – yet it is sweet enough

to watch the sun, far off, cut, as with a razor bleeding,
pink-fading, at day's death staining, the sea's edge in the west.

Wires

The wind settles a nervous hum spun looped
at the top of this telegraph pole;
a hub of lively messages
where not so many eyes would think to look.

The spool of untidy wires stretches, swaying,
on to the next one.
It slices the whining wind
to its desolate bone.

At the foot of the pole is sand,
an abandoned tyre, half-buried,
a block of cement, bag-shaped,
hardened by northern rain,

its paper covering long since whipped away.
I walk to the next pole with its gather of swag
and catch the fretted edge of a thin, mournful tune;
following miles of courier wire, a narrow band of road.

Folie

But, oh, you foolish, foolish birds, singing
by the streetlamp and it dark all around.
What makes you so — *folie à deaux* — *folie en masse*?

We, also, who, with bowed heads from grinding toil,
lift, like dandelions attacking the pavement,
seeing hope in so many places — clouds, lambs and sunshine.

From what amnesiac invocation does this blessing
arise or quiver down. From what close mothership?
Let scalpel blades erase all sight of happy stars,

cut all scenarios of future — its rigid tendons —
let this ignorant bird in delusion delight in song,
for I know it is dark but cannot see the flock of stars.

It is the roar of dinosaur, the grunt of bear, no more.
Let their wilderness songs also fill city streets,
as my transient heart-throbs tick the beat.

What Have You Been Doing?

Come, what have you been doing to yourself?
Let me fix a wiper for your glistened eyes,
bandage up some leaks, renew your brakes;
you have been freewheeling dangerously,
skating the ordered streets,
bumping into citizens and pillar boxes,
spilling messages everyone is too polite to read,
except for postcards of course: *Here I stay, safe,*
   it's lovely here, the deep water so blue,
   if you hold this picture to the light,
   I have put a pin through for you,
   you will see where I am.
Oh, you have been jabbing at your own heart again.
You are one of the people who pierce their own hearts.
You must stop...

She Weeps

She weeps in the tangled forest
for every suffering life;
frees strangled flies from webs,
fretting moths stuck to sap, stranded bees, wounded ants.
With single limbs or wings they hobble off...

She might pet a struggling worm and bury it,
then watch a lost chick, famished, dissipate heat in her hand.
To the blind and plaguey rabbit proffering leaves,
she is a terrible angel of anti-death
 − head nurse of a terminal ward she maintains...

I say, do not weep, for the wheel turns
crushing you, me, and butterflies equally all.
But she walks on, anguished and weeping.
Nobody thanks her
and the flowers in her hair...

Silently screaming.

Daffodils

In this cold twilight of a February
day has not much of a meaning
to these thin, poor, stretched daffodils,

attenuated beyond normalcy or mercy
in the slave-isles of the Scillies,

forced into buds and traded in dozens,
rubber-banded, boxed and scarce alive,

they will never even feel the tender
Spring they promise

drooping fraily in my vase;
gifts unlikely to open

but still, like Van Gogh's sunflowers,
humanistic in their poses:

They dance their greetings, die and flop;
worn out like young limp prostitutes.

At last all lean bent not towards the pale window,
but to the only heat source here –
the fire, the hot coals, the yellow scorch of flames.

Teresa

Her eyes capture like spikes piercing
the gathering drift of his starkest thoughts.
And her lips, truth to tell, express
the chiselled scheme of hers better
than the actual words taking plastic shape
a few seconds on.
She is not afraid, this one,
not afraid of losing him,
not afraid of speaking her mind.
This isn't going to work, she says, laughing,
but is willing to look at it, this bright revenant.
In her confidence she is not afraid
of contradicting herself
and the swift demure recoil just then
belies the biting kiss she gave him
so sudden his boots filled with glue,
the snakes fell out of his head
and she, so at ease, so still, in the moment,
computing back and forth as only brains know how
and will insist
but only for a little while, not to excess.
She is refreshing to be with, he decides:
Quick, smart – too smart to stupefy herself
with a mess of self-deception as to how
she should or shouldn't be
in this exacting studio we call life.
She is possibly an undiscovered masterpiece, he muses,
not being an expert, of course, more a jobbing carver.
Nonetheless, humming, pleased,
he continues to chip,
fashioning, sculpting, feeling for her form.

Touch

She was with me
yet deep within herself
also
her eyes were hollow
I could see right through
and I saw – what did I see?
A child – and I thought I would be
friends with this wounded child
even solve the conundrum of pain
I was expecting lightning bolts
of happiness
electric rain an applause of birds
perhaps
but she grew into a woman
in front of me
underneath me
through me in me
all this time she was
watching
and each time I reached
to touch
she changed into something
I couldn't.

In Your Stillness

It seems to me that in your stillness you float
enclosed in a complete cloud of ecstasy
that kisses you and when your big black kohl-
lidded eyes snap open they
laser into me your special scowl that dizzies me.

Your perfectly proportioned shape
reminds me of a perfume bottle
cognoscenti might peer into
and pore over longingly,
wanting a dip to taste your scent.

I see you wherever women walk and are pictured;
on palace walls, internal and external,
in top seraglios, on urns,
in breasted foam, by sea-borne men belovèd
and in fashionable boulevards enthralling all

and, bound, I see you writhing, melting,
adrift in sparks your vivid hair
as at witch-catchers you spit, uncaring
and to priests you curse defiant
condemnation that for centuries they burn in their own turn:

Burn and shrivel, dark souled men, craving ever, cursèd
– lusting for your own sisters.

Your hips and lips are just-so slightly swollen
like my throat moaning with desire.
Still unclaimed are you in your dinky cardigan
and flared frock
with tissue clouds surrounding you

that cradle you, caressingly,
beyond your pane of cellophane;
as I would if perhaps to purchase you I dared
– dearest doll, fresh and majestic,
                    gorgeous in your box.

The Thing in the Corner

She comes in, ignoring the thing in the corner.
Quickened by that connection, it squirms and begins to stir.
She pours a glass of wine. It starts to beg.
She clicks and switches, opens packets, turns on artefacts.

She slumps on cushions, flicks through magazines.
Pictures and headlines barely make it to her brain.
She has been labouring and needs some rest.
But the thing in the corner won't let her.

This is now a test: Shall we let her doze on the sofa,
as toast-smoke creeps its acrid way along the walls?
I should like to waken her from listlessness.
The angel in the corner growls.

The Prestidigitation of Landscape

The vista unravels away to the distance,
like a crinkled parchment map.
It shudders a little as it unpeels.

I have taken this view home before to cosset
and I return it super-imposed now
fastened into place. I pick a few rocks and tumble them

to a new spot, unpack an alert rabbit there;
this, my personal vision board – I reach
for that fuzzy bird in the corner,

sharpening up its wing curve, change the omen;
straightening trees, my fingers pluck a few,
just for fun, my palm slaps out a clearing

to put you in. Now must I content you:
Is this little brook a pleasure?
Would you, perhaps, prefer this river

ribboning through the guarded plain
of smooth mosses and grass, a clear sky,
where I have set aside a camp, a fire pit...

But I see that you have shifted
and you dance to a harsh, bold flute
in a ring of stone I didn't bring or expect.

Dream

Pouring the tea,
she tells her dream.
He listens, kind of,
busy with his lap-top machine.
Listen, I was in this community...
Oh, right, then, that old dream again.
No, but this time we had all arrived at once...
Like at boarding school?
No, we were grown-ups, it was a five-day workshop...
And I suppose you were the outcast again?
Goddammit yes, but I was admired and loved...
For your odd-ball quirkiness, I guess?
Yes, but dammit, listen: they were giving out sheets...
But you didn't get one, right?
Shut up, I couldn't even get a bed,
I missed meal-time, got separated,
then got lost in the gardens outside
till somebody finally took an interest in me.
This e-mail is definitely spam.
Are you listening?
Yes, you found somebody else
      – in your dreamy garden.

Jungle Room

Here, where you thought safe
is suddenly
dangerous

it is too late to unzip your words
they are all
spilled out

and the wrong answer is embedded
too firmly
to change

it was a trap you fell for
a test
you failed

and now the hunter will rip your heart out
and eat it
in front of you

and suddenly you have lost your appetite
for this game
back to square one

for she is many squares ahead of you
mistress of ladders
you in the pit.

A Walk in the Park

Like the double savage uproot of an ingrown hair
so edifying to remember
the ending of our brief affair
her in weak sunlight wandering the park
her green velvet walking jacket cinched at the waist
disagreement over world news the inner state
it represents – *I just can't share your particular hates
and fears* – I have my own disputed islands
like emergence of that mob's *idée fixe*
switches on my panic mode
and memories of bad dreams – running
always running from secret thought police
in some bad-ass dictatorship

We stop to admire an eroded pinnacle of stone
studded with cypress and saxifrage
an outcrop of wildlife – a clever squirrel –
he knows how to spin and strip a nut
I have fed this one before called City Sid
he eats chestnuts straightaway but buries hazels
– something about endurance of casing I guess
and she picks up and deposits in my hand
a cold pale egg of an unknown bird
now this raises a whole new lot of questions
I hope she is not demanding compassion
sooner or later we all come up against and broach
some sacred fetish – the white scar the red line
we each contain our own righteous army

Beleaguering the fortress of the other – pelt and smash
everything we notice like a shameful lack of feathers
or slow majestic weeping pine loping away from wind
or the disclosure of a never-before-seen nut
slips like a fixed note a tuning fork into the world's brain
I cannot conceive the pitiless tenacity
required for true randomisation
old patterns once again coagulate like resin
so it is meant to be then that we just take hands and hug
and stick to safer subjects avoiding blood
from invisible thorn creating a meaning
from *out* of itself like as answer I tell the story
of a smarty professor of philosophy
who challenges me to prove the existence of a tree
and I say *What tree?*

Downsizing

The first to go was the wok
in its box – with all its silly
folderols. Then, the fondue set.
Next, a glass ornament, a jug,
shifty dishes at the bottom of the pile. Towels
started disappearing. Two
unnecessary chairs moved away
in the night.

Then I noticed your hair was less
and the twinkle in your eyes
and your cheek! Hollowed.
And your bum was definitely smaller
and your waist pinched.

All the things I hadn't touched
in years, weeks, minutes,
were disappearing into holes,
my own lips...

Lovewalk

I want to take you for a walk.
I will carry you respectfully
at heart level so you may know
the nearness of my heart.

I will encase you in a cage of ribs
of woven willow so you might enjoy
protection as we amble through brambles
and thorns and mulch of leaves

and fallen limbs of trees,
the broken bark and mushroom reek
filling the morning air.
Do not be afraid,

I am not going to bury you
in the living waste of forest floor,
nor will I hang you on a branch
to be pecked by birds.

See, I cup you in my hands:
you in your containment
as you swell with intelligent interest
wondering why the need to love

is so strong and complex.
As I place you on an ivy-covered log
and wave goodbye
you climb between the bars and fly.

And As I Wait I Tremble

These plates are floating, though I know
they shouldn't be.
The buildings lean in, lowering
over the street.
Cobbles rush their ancient patterns.
Windows are eyes, but
lashless. Their cords rattle
and the dancing stars crowd down
like lemmings
in the dark ink-blue.

I wait for you
in this raffish café
at the edge of town.

Thin, the moon, poignant, thin,
its blade cuts at my heart.
And I think you may be late.

I Depress Myself on My Coffee Break

I press the plunger on my coffee.
The sun seems to stride through cloud, brightens
and lightens with its golden fingers.
Such a fancy. Summoning energy,
I click the redundant light switch off.
The clock on the wall ticks on.
This is the plain accounting of my life
I requested.

There is enough material here to scavenge
– a lifetime. My pencil poises on Sudoku.
At this moment the kitchen dresser with its stains
carries a message. *Wait*, it says.
You don't walk in.
Cradling the cup, I sip, bribe the clock
to silence and express the well-felt substance
of my squeezed and straining heart.

They Never Met

They never met,
they never kissed,
they never viewed the moon together
perched on ivied walls in forest mist.

They never met,
they never gasped,
as stars took shape
in velvet night,

to see the sun
gulped slow by sea
and, dragon-like, with claws of red,
emerge again at dawn to warm their breasts.

They never met to lick the same spoon,
to stitch each others' hearts
to the backs of hands,
wrists offered up to the binding of ribbons.

They never met.
It was never like this; it was never like this:
That they, urgent, moaning, lay,
in each others' arms.

They passed each other often in the street,
brushed coats, but never met.
they never met: it was never like this:
Kiss-shock soft-tender on bed of moss stretched.

They never looked, they never knew,
that they were both coloured blue
and so they lived and so they died,
never meeting, me and you.

Shedding *(A Fantasie)*

Shedding tears is old hat.
There is nothing so original in that.
And those drops, with all my nervous sweat,
are usefully slaking starveling plants. But look –

Questing bees pluck the once precious love-words
from my mouth to scatter them like puffballs
around this pale, passionless garden.
Swelling, they spill their stale, sour spore.

And now I'm stripped of flirty glances,
pretending to admire blades of grass,
they writhe among a heap of hugs,
embarrassing the chickweed there.

I am shifting stock, downsizing, getting
lighter – there, I just got rid of a dozen smiles,
little scimitars piercing earth,
a barrow-load of discarded handshakes,

hundreds of kisses landing to suck
on the bark of indifferent trees.
And caresses – Oh, there they go swooping high,
wasted on the jackdaws in the leaves above.

And don't talk to me about hearts on sleeves.
Mine has just floated off on a deep stream,
its warm wake attracting lusty things that follow,
hunting and biting like in a solid dream.

I Try to Bring Order

Of course, poor old Dormouse,
he's nodded off again:
narcoleptic – mid phrase –
cup and saucer poised in left hand,
quivering only slightly, whiskers and breath...
I glued them all together (not the 'tache)
to help him out – there – he comes back round
...*when I was in Kashmir...*
and Hatter droning on about hats,
completely spaced;
Oh yes, a few bowlers for the Yankee tourists,
but the trade is all in fascinators these days,
bobbing bits of feathers and fluff,
you see, people just won't pay the money
for a proper Panama...
Panama? Hare jolts up ears,
I was stuck on a boat once in Panama
– damn terrorists – couldn't get a woman for weeks
or was that Suez? Hmm...
His testosterone-fuelled paw fumbles absently
with Alice's knees under the tablecloth.
And how is your claim going,
enquires Alice politely of Hatter,
regarding the chemical poisoning?
Time to move, time to move, Dormouse pipes up,
almost stumbling into the big brown Betty.
We should really get a dishwasher, Alice remarks.
You are *the dishwasher,* laughs Hare,
pulling at her pretty purple sash.
I find a fresh seat in the shuffle,
fondling the silver thimble in my pocket.
And Time and his cohort, Déjà Vu, must surely smile
as I pour the thick cold tea
and all turn to stone, looking at me.

Dolly

Fear is the presence
of the doll's eyes
snapped wide and staring
open and   shut
in an instant's blink
according to elevation
the child must learn the trick of
or be terrified
of those patient eyes
remonstrating in between
comforting in tones
learned from mummy
if those eyes are not
controlled they will take hold
of a life of independence
which means for example
knocking on the toy box at night
or playing dead
or rattling cup 'n saucer
or worse malfunctioning
with a hideous wink
of doll-like knowingness
that the tea party is fake
and the whole thing

Mummy, Why Is That Man...?

Here a little girl squats, fascinated,
the more to view a very huge man draped
in army camouflage. He sleeps on the pavement
with a blanket, sign, fat rucksack and cap
of scattered coins.
He is willing to work, it says.

When she gets home she commands
her regiment of dolls
to lie down.
She makes sure their eyes are sealed shut
and constructs little signs for them,
placing coins from her
plastic post office kit
in front of each

Then wakes them up and, with brisk words,
sets them to work
– tidying the house, pouring tea...
She keeps all the coins.

Flotsam

The children play in plastic flotsam
on the beach.
The tides have washed it in
with lines of brackish sedge,
smelly shells, crab pots, rope,
love dolls, sandals, lighters.
I specialize in floats, myself.
Others collect kinder toys or balls.
There are more and more life-jackets these days.
Their whistles are highly prized.

At night the whole strand is ghostly.
Lobsters wave antennae through the cage bars,
flip-flops once again nudge goals in graceless arcs,
moanings and gasps arise from haunted heaps
of shredded cord and wormy wood,
stink of shared old cigarettes,
friends and lovers tangle, their eyes glacial,
dogged in groups, among wrecked boats,
stubbornly unquenchable in their rank quest for refuge.
And the bulging life vests shiver and creep in wind.

The Adult Carousel

This is not a children's ride;
a ratty ring of bells and buses;
not a squatty little roundabout
for toddlers.
Why, no, these comely horses big and wild,
have stirrups, straps of studded leather, bridle bits
and hair from dead trapeze acrobats.
They are double-saddled so that sweethearts
can embrace and squeeze as they go
up and down
up and down
round about at boisterous speed.

But at night once when I was small
and all was cloaked and still, and I,
hushed and on watch peeking thrust
through spokes of a caravan wheel
saw one of the horses twitch his tail
and jerk his mane and he was off
and then another and another
and as each jumping horse leapt free
the impetus nudged the carousel backwards
a little more strongly until it was empty
except for the smell of the sweat of animals
and barley-twisted poles
pumping and spinning,
spinning and pumping,
at crazy angles.

And the horses snorted smoke and galloped all away
until my father tempted them with metal hay
to calm them down and and get them back
and persuade them that one day
he would set them free in a meadow forever.

Spun like Candy

Earthy smell of onion, meat and piccalilli in a bun,
sweet alchemy of sugar powder spun to fluff.
I'm hanging out with my new friend, Suzy,
at the cheapest thrill in town – Penny Heaven –
where money crashes down for free sometimes
and all you have to do is wait
for gravity and luck.

We had a firm kiss by the dodgems – senses assaulted:
Sparks, ozone, stink of tortured metal.
We gripped each other as the pumping horses thrust,
watching riders mesmerized to stone,
then decided to blow five on the waltzers
and as the first, slow, undulating grind began,
the cheeky ride-boy stayed with us

shoving us extra gratuitous heaving twists,
getting off on my girlfriend's screams
and receding skirt while I, what to do,
what can I do but grin the rictus grin,
determined to enjoy the vicious spin relentlessly
twirling, humping, right up until the end he gives us
one final shove, the jerk, we are the last to stop...

Her surprised eyes. Her creamy thighs.
Skirt ridden high. Prepped by a hard fair-boy.
This defilement hot and sweaty just for me,
delicious as peaches pressed in a pie,
sweet and sticky, spun like candy.
We stagger off, delirious, arm in arm,
squirming through the currents of moneyless teenagers...

The Piano Demolition Display

At the County Show,
four doughty men with hammers, gloves and goggles
stand prepared in dramatic pose.
At blare of klaxon the smash begins.
First, the wooden case, thin veneer of walnut
and fretwork, too delicate for steely lumps on poles,
over-stretched with clumsy wasted force. The men pause,
baffled by their unsubtle strength, then gang up on
the ivory splinters of long-dead elephants
but, again, the unspectacular crush
of weak, glued artefact
and the mob laughs at the sounds struck
– a mocking, clownish disharmony.
Frazzled now and sweaty, the men turn to
the exposed frame of strings,
the naked heart of piano;
a solid over-strung under-damper Bechstein.
At last the men exult.
This is man's work.
Iron on iron. Crash.
There go the F-sharps, the Gs and high Cs;
augmented fifths, A-minor chords, the last
the piano will ever play
and she gasps as the cast metal cracks.
Oh this is worse, far worse
than the innocent pounding of naughty children.
A whiplash of B curls and cuts a chest,
the man yells, takes it out on the pedals
while the others finish her off.
The brass twinkles in the sun. The crowd claps.
The Tannoy announces next the judging of the bulls.

Merrie England

There is some epic scamper going on down
the hill of tradition – boiled eggs, wheels of cheese,
whole damn barrels of flaming pitch,
crowds held back by fluorescent stewards,
tourists recording movies for YouTube,
shaky as the buckets rattled for cancer,
thumping yokels, shin-kicking farmers,
grunting modern hero folk-jesters...
and afterwards, the race to the pub.

Propping up the Swan and Musket saloon bar,
with deep and wormy antique cracks,
over-fed protein-stuffed chaps bump skulls
on Elizabethan smoked-oak beams and ingle-nooks;
dusty, low, spidery, studded with knick-knacks;
poisonous pewter, brass oddities, lacquered iron,
blades and spikes, obscene instruments,
bubbling with cruelty, rust and spite;
a chaos of feathers, antlers and varnished fish.

The supreme relic hangs above me:
manacles from africa, enough for three
black slave necks joined by rigid poles.
The fools, the fools! Why did they not
destroy it when they had the chance?
My eye is transfixed on a trap for moles.
The ale and cider fumes fug my head.
My fingers hoist out the last cheesy crisp
and as the minstrels fine-tune mandolins, I exit quick.

The Executioner Relaxes at Home

When the executioner relaxes from his task,
nights at home, does he remove his mask
or keep it on to govern wife and child by fright
 – groom them straight and uniform,

squinting through his eye-holes like a mole
scanning moral newspapers
aloud for them with pious yarns
of knaves, remorse and retribution?

Does he fabricate with matchsticks
model scaffolds,
play at hangman with his son
 – spelling useful words like 'bulge' and 'strangulated'?

Does he slip his woman extra when he's had a busy day,
dream of clients twitching in his bed,
mewling into her armpit
and she must comfort him as like a babe?

At least I think on Sundays he must doff it
so as to trim moustache and eat some beef,
spruce himself for Monday's work.
That must be such a relish and relief!

In The Soldiers' Comfort Camp

A dozen hungry tongues and fingers
lick and scrape in every pot.
We lodge in one living unit,
which had wheels once that worked.
Now only we work – for our meals.
It is a blessing when one dies.
We try to hush it up three days
before bad smell betrays us
and we get our replacement
work and meal sharer.
Meals and work.
Work and meals.
That's about it, really.
That is our lot.
There are no showers (that old lie),
only the blessèd rain
and the warm towel of the sun's rays
to rub us dry.

Playtime in Hell

The red-rimmed eyeballs of cruel men
that once were babies,
crawling among their mothers' pots and pans,

now stare, thrilled, at the
woman they have just impaled,
fascinated by the way her eyes roll.

Her lips, as if tranced,
murmur deprecations;
the harshest judgements ever made on men and boys.

Erupting, her spirit has fled to a quivering star,
unravelled like a string of magician's bright scarves.
Her insides empty. Her body lolls.

These creatures must walk still the flat earth,
making the rocks tremble: Chunks of sky fall,
their breasts heave like monster trolls.

So Normal, So Good, You Look

I can pretend the rhythmic hiss of tyres on tarmac
is the sough of wind in trees.
That swaying trucks are not delivered here.
That scrunching boots in gravel is a beast of innocence
browsing for berries in the woods.
That contrails in the reddening sky
are tracks of angels chasing demons.
I can fake it that the buzz of cogs and gears
is made by the serenades of wasps and bees,
that the spatter of spent bullets
is raindrops
and whack of whips and shouts – are they jeers?
Part of a contest's friendly bit of fun
– properly refereed, with whistles
and that yelling kids are merely yelling kids.
In the playground, yellow smoke is burning leaves
and silent birds are only tired
and all around, the crisp and fried black grass
is meant to be like that.
And twisted words off acid lips are all correct and true.
But to see you standing, hanging there
clean and clear on that other side of wire.
So normal, trim and neat you look, so good, like a dream.
You open your mouth but no sound issues.
– *Are you real?* I silently scream.

Another Dead Soldier

This dead one was *not* a golden boy,
not the dearest father in the world,
not the lovingest husband one would long for,
no, nor the brightest soul in a village that will still,
probably, empty for his funeral.
No, he was thick, cruel, and belligerent, one who
would torment then shoot prisoners if he could.

He just disappeared in the crud of a road bomb
one hot fluid morning with his mates patrolling.
The papers will locate someone to lie
and re-write what a good guy he was. No, nobody
really liked him ever, but, he was a soldier:
The flag flew low for him one evening,
the bugle blew, and the sergeant saluted.
Better this way, dead, this one.
Better this way dead, this son.

At the Truth and Reconciliation Commission Amnesty Hearings

Yes, I admit, many. In custody
they were there to be raped.

Yes, I tortured to extract truth.
I used water and electric whips.

Once, just to shut it while I upset its mother,
I shattered a baby's head on my desk.

I am a normal soldier but regret
that I have never fought a foreigner.

I have been taught to perform not to feel.
Is it enough to say sorry now?

What if I offer to strip myself
of this, our country's uniform,
pull off these disgraced epaulettes,
the appalling stripes and medals,
melt my buttons, make a
bitter monument of shame
for all to spit on
and renounce my amnesty?

In the hot, restless, aching courtroom
where hungry justice was being fed,
slow drip by slow drop,
and tense freedom purchased with
the untested, newly invented
law of confession,
in my stern dream, in crazy fantasy,
the colonel says all that and
unpredictably claws back into
a sort of man again – earning what?
A tentative applause?

The Roses Of Heliogabalus

And the paradox of damnatio memoriae

They hang by the ceiling, soft and limp;
cartloads of roses, threshed from the tyrant's fields.
their dense weight settled, they breathe on the feast.

Their celestial scent pervades the air,
mingled with earthy smells of dormice stuffed
in the kitchen with pork-paste and pine nuts;

boiled ostrich, flamingos and parrots,
musky sweat of oiled dwarf wrestlers,
delicate perfumes of luxury dancing girls...

As they work through the menu to dessert – the *secundae*,
the emperor, Heliogabalus, gives a great belch
and on a wave of his big royal hand, the roof-gates collapse

expelling their ambush of costly surprise:
And as the chosen ones inhale with their choked-off sighs,
petals, light as the breath they put a stop to,

mixed with spilt wine and trampled dates and honey cakes,
do they recognise, these guests, they are the top-billed wonder
stars of this night's scandalous, unforgotten cabaret?

Crimescene

The archaeologists sift through the hill,
puzzled by their redactive spoils;
baffled by anachronistic mixtures of sherds
and a gaggle of infant teeth far from a jaw...

I could tell them:
all those broken grins were mine;
the red-streaked milk-bones collected as they dropped
by a loving mother hoarded in a long-rotted purse

and those cups and plates and jars were gathered
by an antiquarian father who loved to hold
artefacts of those who went before us,
much like the men who excavate now the destruction...

which came in the evening
too suddenly swift for me
to decipher the meaning
of the screams...

on luminous nights I would be seen as I bent
moonbeams – twisting between dour tussocks –
the occasional leery peasant careful
to not look too hard...

how I rejoice now in the trench-slits of de-sutured earth,
skittering over trestled evidence like an eel,
feeling original foundations, fire-blackened stones,
beginning to sleep more, caring not for your verdict...

Statue Unearthed

One arm is missing, some toes;
yet noble still, the face remains, with chipped nose.
Your laurelled stony curls survive
the catastrophe that hid you,
consumed your marble whole,
reclaiming very soon those minerals
that painted you; the ochres and umbers
that tinted you – the slight swell of abdomen,
coloured your cheeks, your eyes,
that now stare blank into the two-thousand-years-later sun...

We will not give you eyes, nor freshened nose,
we moderns, nor prosthetic arm.
Our fashion is to honour that plain damage as antique.
This second life of yours is bonus, we believe
and then, we, who value history,
will expose, on some museum's stage,
all those stains and gross wounds suffered,
labelled with your provenance and status,
the long dead flesh you represent,
until Time spirals back with fresh floods of destruction:

The last attendant that could defend you gone,
no priest-curator to attest to your preciousness,
that this rock-carved revenant deserves fate better
than reburial in silt and ash below,
smothered with the unguarded treasure
of all our ruined houses,
but safe at least from dim barbarians above
with their grim, twilight message
and savage rubble
– hammering all the statues for their hard and stony god.

What I Do for You

Do you know what I do for you?
I chip and shape, with my teeth I scrape
at this great artefact of mine.

I drag it from my cave to show you
what my workshop has achieved.
You send it back along the groove I've made.

I consider something more wheel-like may please you;
it would certainly be easier to move.
It's getting smaller though

with each rebuff. Do you realize
this is the shrine of my people you reject;
this beautiful soul I labour to sculpt

in the darkness of my cave.
Do you know how hard it is to make
a hollow stone?

It rings.
Yes, strike it.
It rings for the blind.

The Rabbit Pleads for Acceptance

The rabbit was desperate to impress:

The cat always feeds on our brains first
– oughtn't that, doesn't that, tell you something?
And regard the magnificence of our tunnelled architecture:
Cosy, communal, ventilated, safe;
integral with protocol for entrance and exit;
back-door evacuation systems built in...

He would nibble on carrots dreamily proclaiming
that abstract vegetable sculpture was a measure
of a wholly sublime peak civilisation.

Once I caught him in a sunbeam absorbed
completely in the art of shadow puppetry.
With convoluted ears and paws he made
a very passable replication
of a human hand.

The religious fervour of his courage
based upon regular sacrifice
to the sacred headlamps in duality
was, he assevered, a proof beyond question
of the spirituality of the rabbit nation.

My people cast pellets in Fibonacci spirals,
divinate in dance the very geometry of fate
that accords with the patronage of stars;
on dew-wet tracks we leap, creating scintillant fractals,
dodging snares, communicating complex revelations
with the bright flashing bobs of our semaphoring tails,
and who, oh you rare fools, do you imagine manifests
those manufactured conundrums of what you call crop circles?

He gathered himself, twitching, heart and breath...
I was more than a little impressed, myself, if not scared,
but the others were not willing to incorporate the rabbit race
– the *oryctolagus cuniculus* –
into the commonwealth of all enlightened beings
and being also famished, shot him.

Eagles

I can perceive a rabbit more than two miles away
but this is much too easy prey for her.
Sometimes, when chasing a fox, say,
she, my mate, will course and zig-zag
until the bush-tailed beast is exhausted;
the pathetic wight tries to bury itself,

then I, golden raptor of the skies,
swoop in for the good-time kill.
She is magnificent, Aquila, my mate;
her wings stretch to an even wider span than mine
– more than one of your six-foot troopers.
Grim and pitiless she governs and culls,

despising my habit of eating dropped tortoises,
insisting there is no art there at all.
She just cannot honour that beautiful sport;
the matching of carapace to perfect target stone.
She reminds me, with mocking screech, of old, bald Aeschylus,
whose untimely death...but, no matter...

We rest, replete, full of heart and ham, digesting...
We witness your antique standards, your inspired empires,
pleased and flattered by respectable reflections;
the homage of your metal money, stitched flags, your temples,
chiselled with our images, those wholesome values you adopt
– you Romans, you young Americans, you Hittites, you Nazis...

I Ladle the Hours, Dispense the Days

I know I am just a thing,
but my master needs me: He looks at me often
through the glass, he checks the whereabouts
of my hands. (It pleases him to call them thus).
My heart is mechanical but is driven by
a 1.5 volt double A battery:
Reliable. Rechargeable.
I tick, therefore I am.

My owner needs to know when to
drink coffee, get up, sit down, make lunch,
Keep appointments and so forth.
I deliver, divide and split.
Sometimes he chides himself
for some perceived disparity
between the workings of his own heart and mine:
Goodness me, look... he will say and then
invoke the Sacred Name of My God.

He is becoming a convert.
I am taming his wild, clock-less, pagan ways.
I motivate and steady him.
He never blames me for what passes:
He is more concerned about that reflector thing
hanging above me. He frowns at her.

I dole out the minutes, ladle hours,
sprinkle seconds, dispense days, cut wedges of weeks
and see! How brisk the measured months cascade
coalescing effortless to sweeps of years
– silt of centuries!

But she above me knows nothing of this.
She is irreligious, shows only the moment
that denies and abnegates my sweet God;
invokes only the shameless present.

But look how now he teases himself.
He holds me up to that deceiving bitch.
– Fancies I now go backwards...

Bubble

The carpenter scrapes and sands and he squints
till I sit, balanced, between two black lines;
freakish, a trapped exhibit;
like a fly up against a window pressed.

They stained her green,
though she is no chartreuse,
this gravity addicted alcohol
and I, from my freedom, randomly grabbed.

We tell them which way up to go, what kilter to obey.
It is our clash and argument strikes the true.
We are inimical, spirit and I.
Ever am I rising from her weak grasp.

I have been places you wouldn't credit,
been the vital soul in bread and blood and beer,
compressed in tubes to power God knows what fiendish machines
and I have frolicked long with fishes' gills below the wave.

Like a bottled genie, I rage,
baleful behind verdant glass.
Yet my character has grown in gaol, I notice things;
this dusty mess; the shaved curls, artful skills,

obsessive men compelled to set the tilted world aright.
For I am emperor of order in my bubbledom,
the oracle of doors well hung,
the arbiter of casements, of flat, level shelves.

Once, the foreman's scamp of a child
took me up and shook and shook
till I turned to stars
and all my fragments swirled like hurricane,

reminding me of sky and all the drops we used to make
from the vast wet essence of our being
till they fell as rain
scattered and shattered upon the earth.

Weather House

For S.W. & S.T.

I am the boy, she that girl,
in this rustic weather house,
conjoined together by a simple twist of gut,
its baleful twirl propelling me, with Alpine hat,
into the inclement grey

and *she* glides out quite easily
with her pretty parasol,
vibrating to sunbeams, I guess,
sensing her form from behind as I loiter in our hut,
waiting with longing for her return.

But when she does come back, of course, I get this crazy urge
to check out the sky and its clouds and moods,
so overcome am I by the movements of her person
in that complete tragical distance
that never can we bridge.

Often and often, we meet at the edge, all smiles,
as though in a fugue, with such minuscule trembles,
pivoting on the threshold of a tentative day,
until that cruel sinew takes a quarter turn, perhaps,
and one of us departs.

Pinioned with pain for my Gretchen I can never touch,
as opposites we puppets jerk, compelled to dance;
as weather slaves we swivel by
to gristle's wretched whims, in cursèd minuet,
my wooden heart in knots convulsed, each time the sky turns blue.

Cats Eyes

Keep your lights on, pray,
I depend that you do this,
I am strange that way.
I sleep by day and doze at night until
your bright machine sweeps by
which I reflect, my glitter eyes
a warning guide,

illuminating humps and curves
and dangerous bends for you.
If you must overtake I will retract,
rumbling into my rubber shoes,
I am designed for that.
But can you stand for long the pounding beat,
that squelchy pulpy sound as you change lanes?

And, though not common, it may be,
one eye of mine might pop and rupture.
Do not swerve to follow it.
Some gutter child will most likely
approach the lure,
marvel at its thick glass simplicity,
and discover at home its torched awakening.

And so, then, my can-opening friend,
as you journey, this side for you, this side not,
my cats eyes will be watching out for you,
straight dead-centre on the road.
Do not deviate, my speedy friend,
keep your boundaries;
the soft meat of you, cradled in your tin.

God of the Pencil Box

Sometimes there is nothing to do,
just lie straight in the pencil box,
slotted with all the others,
sensing the comfort of the eraser
in his compartment – our guide and friend –
compassionate provider of the second chance.

He is in fact God of the pencil box,
you have to pressure very hard to beat him.
The coloured ones only are immune;
they create gay, indelible rainbows and such,
while we draw shadows and edges,
monumental buildings, grey rain.

Today while I was filling in
four dozen slate tiles on a steeple
of a superlative cathedral,
the point of my being just
snapped.

God sent the sharpener
and allowed me to enter her.
Somebody, then, I don't know who,
twisted...

Fable

At last, God broke through.
Into a gap in the blue he cantered.
Yes, he came and entered the single chapel,
keeping the faith still, with priest and people:

And God declared himself to that congregation
chanting and kneeling on needlepoint cushions,
slotted in high latched pews
wearing their finest clothes.

Outside and placid, was the entourage.
Angels on horseback rustled and breathed in
that sweet meadowy essence of flowers
which gladly surrendered, one by one, their lives.

Inside it was mayhem and outrage: God was bound
and stapled to the bell and rung and the dull clang all day
lured locals up the holy hill and the priest press-ganged them
into the freshly revived New Church of Resurrection.

As horses turned dejected heads from the din,
the angels forever renounced their religion
 – jealousy of the human form and its divinity –
and went diverse ways in no sure direction.

When the Gods Went

When the Gods went
they did not take everything
but left behind in dining halls
of obsidian pillars and porphyry floors,
flakes of gold paint and lapis peeling from frescoes
recounting metamorphic intercessions
committed at their pleasure, unrestrained
and, littering palaces everywhere,
their mountains, grottoes and forest glades,
all their accoutrements:

Hammers, javelins, helmets,
spinning wheels and harps and engines,
kept up to date and best quality for their times,
in the noumenal glory of their prime.
But those things were not buried
as with mortal kings and queens,
for Gods do not die, as such,
they fade and diminish to a hint of auras,
meagre and hollow, too weak to carry
divine equipment or wear majestic cloth,

which, with their chequered histories, decays at last,
evaporating essence like their owners,
all descending, like dismantled rainbows, to a parched earth.
The covetous and poetic may catch godly remnants;
at edges of clouds, faces in flowers, bloody sunsets,
your twin reflected in a black and bitter lake,
sudden race of leaves, groan of oak, echo of stag,
frost turned to smoke in the morning sun,
newspaper loud headline announcing:
Woman Raped By Animal.

At the Seaside

A woman, aching to escape her world,
divides herself. A mound of doughy baps unwrapped,
she muses on the soft, rolling structures out there,

where pink, floppy limbs, in crumbling dunes, flail.
She smears oily gold, lays on some slippy ham,
as boys and girls disport with a wobble ball.

She cuts tomatoes firmly
with a sharp serrated edge.
A toe could be sliced by broken whelk shell or splint of glass.

A boiled egg, a twist of salt, was how it used to be.
She never liked the taste of sea. From a jar,
she dollops on mayonnaise, sprinkles cress. Screeching,

the kids hurl seaweed as furious gannets dive,
protecting their young. In pain from headache,
she worries about all babies – drowning,

in their little sun-dresses.

Swaddling sandwiches in the rented hut,
the table-scape littered with detritus, stranded,
on the beach, like plastic bags, countless blobs of jellyfish.

Blowzy blow-flies zig-zag on random breeze,
following their noses through the greasy screen of beads.
The rock shadows she is enticed by, will of course stink

of the living and the dead; piss and deceased crabs.
Those prawns she bought as a treat for herself are off
and that crude squabble with gulls over ice-creams was grotesque.

On the walls, pictures of tugboats and schooners.
Imagining sailors sunk in wet sleet storms,
she hauls up beaded bottles from the ice box

and purses lips, swats wasps, calls out a summons,
nervous of the sandy chaos to come
but clutches tight her thermos, parasol, and her reading:

a book about Schrödinger's cat, worm-holes in the fabric
of space and time and the infinite splitting
of universes.

Fetching My Love Back

The path unravelled itself in low grass,
brown, as though from a poison dripped
from a narrow cart containing casualties
– men and women yoked in sorrow,
crammed together, in their failure, as keen wind whipped.

But this was a mere conjecture of vision – I was alone
and I saw shoots on either side like green glitter
– mythic signs of hope. I was fetching someone.
I held a promise arranged some time ago
when I made a bargain with Love.

~

I cannot tell much of that hard place,
only I recall the bleak rock walls were worn so smooth
as if fingered and stroked for eternity.
The mood was not of potent threat but tired, flat despair.
It took effort to remember to breathe.

But I beckoned her and she followed, unrestrained,
beyond trust, unafraid and uncomprehending.
She would take up the threads of allure I laid for her,
tracing the tracks back to the country of song and sky,
and she, so frail and quiet, uncertainly behind me...

The path bent and because of that I was tempted
yet stood irresolute at first ... but my passion burst then
like a desperate fruit, unplucked on a lonely tree.
Of course I looked back, of course I did. Even now I look back
to see her resistless form once more consumed by shadow.

Garden

Granting us space, I leave the veranda,
where you preside like a marble queen.
I fix my eye on the butterfly zone
at the far end of the garden.

We are enclosed and, it seems, quite alone,
perhaps no other visitors today.
I caress a wall with its weeping grapes.
It radiates the built-up heat.

A trickling waterfall soothes senses,
alleviates echoes of your complaints.
I loiter by the disjoint sundial,
then skirt the maze I know so well

to the central pond of disagreement,
forsaken but for a tin flamingo,
a brace of nymphs coated with egg-white,
to encourage lichen and moss,

the way you like things – distressed and semi-wild,
in this fey, fantastical romance you make.
I favour koi carp and you want frogs
– and tadpoles are a fishfeast, yes.

Avoiding the thicket of untame thorn,
I withdraw to my palace of flowers,
which you raid, I know, with sharp secateurs,
coveting my amaryllis

to be draped on the statues of Flora,
of Titania and Proserpina.
On those stone effigies, offered wreaths wilt,
while you sing in your fluted dress.

I will command scraped, then, a new mini-lake for you
and lay an antique tulip in your lap.
The black or the blue is my privilege to choose
– because I am the gardener.

Embroidered Garden After Rain

I settle you in the gazebo with your sewing
launching into the sharp garden air for a stroll
we have had the sort of rain that spatters

waxy leaves in patterns of their trailing threads
down silvery birch and satin roses
collecting pictures in a composed world of drops

as your curved needle stitches linen at the edges
shreds of oleander's cut wet petals clog
the culverts' sinewy twists and twines of water

but those difficult showers unattempted by your yarns
the clouds stylised as on a Chinese plate or vase
and mists inchoate even your keen eye cannot capture

and you pat your work flat in hoop of wood
trapped we have watched the pearly beadlets wrinkling windows
now clean-washed as the bleached-white napkin cloth

filling up fast with burdened flowers and trees
and they all have drunk their fill the soaked grass
thirsty no more the artistry of birds

singing ragged songs refreshed
oiled feathers fibrillate with joy on mossy twigs
slickly reproduced with umber and emerald

exquisite and neat as delicate teeth bite taut rayon
colour worms layered in tamed precisely trimmed as you make
my bruising footprints on lawn a sudden different green

a wisp of rainbow guides me silkily through foliage
pulls me back to that hateful wheelchair where deft fingers
resurrect all the purples of your broken tulips.

Artist

Nothing is unbeautiful to artists:
You taught me that with the rigor mortis
of your work.
It is the truth of now, you say
and I collect for you, on the beach,
the artefacts of man and nature,
dreaming of the little boat we used to sail,
shattered now and sunk, the bleached drifted wood,
as you delight in, smooth and wormy.
And I gather for you the endless detritus of sea,
the unpitied carbonate residue of life.
It is all scoured bone, vacant skulls and shells to you,
focused and hunched over lacquered arrangements.
Our love is beginning to stink.
The agates and carnelians I offer turn to matte.
Where is the sparkle?
And the sad sharp glitter of my amber eyes,
how do I harvest that – would you even notice?

And yet, like a dog, I continue to serve you
– the shark egg cases, sponges, the razor clams.
I am tied to you, I fetch lobster pot traps,
fluffed-up orange/blue rope – and bottles, semi-crushed.
You sip rum, cheroot-stained teeth in a grin as I bring
bucket-loads of toothbrushes and lighters.
Do you remember at school the dried starfish and pasta?
That was the start of your singular obsession.
I gave you a ring and you embedded it in resin
with a twist of tagliatelle – and a crab.
You are worshipped for your installations.
Those exhibitions win you acclaim
and I am left behind half-submerged
like a chunk of eroded glass.
What remains for your ironic eye?
A cast off fishing line, roughly cut,
a plastic glove for you to mock,
a washed-up love-doll,
miles and miles of sand.

Brief Sketch of A Ghost Writer

Let us suppose I meet in a café with you,
hatching, perhaps, the half-formed opaque idea
that a lyric could escape, from a hidden spectral place,
slipping over edges of tricks of vision,
past all the remnant wraiths and obstacles laid between us,

the fey, delicate harmony of syllables
visibly swelling as I labour to copy and print,
wishing I could switch to ethereal strokes of brushed thin
pictographic characters to convey quick and timely,
those brief but fertile images I have yet to tell.

Oh how to paint a tune, sing a dance,
to engrave phrases of fragile truth;
as smarter brittle words fade to flickers of film,
dissolved fragments struggling to squeeze through
holes of a skinned reed flute...

Yet as I sit, impatient, waiting for the bill,
hoping to evade the alluring pull
back to the fringes of familiarity,
my grey face etched in mirrors opposite,
it is almost as if they don't want me to go.

Have I become mere artful window dressing,
inertly trapped with empty glass for hours?
As moments stretch unearthly by from melted clocks, I leave
my scheme of coloured song, its buds and skin – a taste
for them and for you also as we separate.

The Visit

I went to visit my friend.
There was a path of sorts
 – bumpy, rocky, rutted.
Flat mandrakes littered the track;
I would ask him about them later
and also about those eaters of the world
who have consumed the future
and I would share my observations
on women. We would meditate upon what lasts.
There was an intelligent shrike
on the wayside calling up newts to impale.
There had been a little light rain
and some snails were slowly ascending;
their enduring shells black and purple
for all to witness in the sun.
Also enduring were the bones of creatures
unknown to me hanging on a walnut tree.
My friend fancied himself as a bit of a shaman
and decorated his shack with grisly items
 – to ward off attack, I guess.
Here now, a clutch of feathers, a red eye
painted on the door,
which opens at my gentle push;
bunches of herbs sway,
sweet and bitter herbs swing.
I have tasted some of these before.
I go no further, he is out.
I sit on a comfortable lump of wood,
gazing at his prayer flags
bisecting the far-off mountain
and placid lake below
and I wait,
my feet in scattered charcoal.

Study of the Object

After Zbigniew Herbert

The object that doesn't exist is most beautiful.
It has no limits or volume or lines,
it does not decay like cheese or wine,
for time has no dominion here,
unlike with furniture, whose damage is ordained
in a disappointing world of splits, cracks and entropy.

Silently, with impossible curse, its aura shrieks,
unperceived, odourless and stiller than a mouse,
willing itself far from predatory gazes,
its contiguous space has no chance to contrast
and emphasise the constraint of its beingness,
so not in the thrall of the daemon of existence,
but now this naked gap commands even more interest
as we come to realise what is missing, astray,
which means, *ergo*, its anti-matter counterpart
is null also and that creates or uncreates
two major holes in the universe – or two minute ones,
it is of no matter – but, in the psyche of mankind,
a void is a nagging ache, one must enlist, choosing,
the contrapuntal spheres of love or hate,
subscribe to the scheme or attract attention,
not always benevolent or welcome.

And the takers, who cannot bear to miss out,
must possess at least an ounce of its essence;
so even as dealers offer promissory notes
to the connoisseurs of ownership,
agencies of governments strive vainly to bomb
the unthinkable into the matrix.

At best it will be assigned a place, *absente reo,*
on an altar, plinth, or display case,
with a script surmising properties,
a plastic model of putative halo, perhaps.
That's it. That's the end story. That's how it is. Or isn't.

I am floating on a raft, struggling with belongings,
after a villainous war of philosophy
and it is circling me, this thing I almost made,
sliming up my punt pole, pretending to be water,
fresh, unsalted, the drink of my dreams.

Or I am a salmon, where plunges a dread waterfall
and this thing, nothing to speak of, is an invisible
spring: Unlocked, unhinged, inside the vortex, I rise,
engineered and shimmering with all the best colours.

Bonfire

It is easy to start: the old-fashioned letters,
the worthless warranties, the pointless guarantees,
every trashy book from holidays we spent.
And the newspapers with useless news.
While the crows cry in the woods regardless.
And oh, the burning leaves of autumn,
I don't have to tell you of that essence.
A box once packed with wrapped possessions
explodes as smoke ignites to flame.
Angry ghosts hiss,
fiddling in the fire.
That broken chair I know so well,
where you and I used to huddle and kiss.
A sweat-stained pillow burns.
Dreams and feathers float
lighter than eyelashes.
I blink from more than smoke.
These are the flakes and artefacts of company;
the cushions of comfort, clothes turned to rags.
I do not disrespect them – there go my shoes,
the heels eroded particle by particle
on every rock and hill and beach I strode,
maddened with the problems of marriage.
And your dress – my favourite dress – cut up.
Long time since it was ironed, I should have kept the buttons.
And the sad curtains full of flowers
and the carpet full of spillage. They sicken me.
They go on top of empty shelves I can no longer fill,
blazing with bright crackle of sparks,
fuelled by dry worm-rot of those years.
It is enough. Time slinks slow as a boulder
oozing into a grave – and I poke
with the tines of a four-pronged fork,
the lump of matted débris – I lift
and the red glares back at me, flares – and settles
to charcoal everlasting;
premonition of the end of ends.
And yet here come the jumping children,
leaping the pit to land in ash,
scratching grey-scale numbers on crazy paving,
playing hopscotch in the erasing rain
and a rainbow creeps across the sky,
forced by the sun.

Cleaning Jane's Stuff

Beginning at the top with feather wand
removing corpses of summer moths
caught in a diabolic mesh
their struggles epic but not enough strength

to save you as I lightly flick ornaments
littering the mantelpiece your shells and healing crystals
useless as the burnt stump of this candle's impoverished
wick engulfed with overflowing wax – oh luckless design.

You were so tiny yet your spirit flame was large.
I lift the ruby vase you loved
deep red contrasting with pale cheek
pictures and photos covered in fine white

ash-dust of the stars they say where you must roam
finally free I trust – a shelf-full of self-help guides
to deal with next, creased and battered
by your invalid chair, button-controlled beneath cushions

an abalone clip for your spindrift hair
the furniture so heavy to shift
and you so frail I carried you
laid you on the carpet there for you to stretch tired bones

– your last yoga pose – and then you curled and died.

Street and the Cellular Split Life of Scenes

...who are the latest to be scaped
shoelaces trail the tricksy pavement
stumping the street walking wandering
up and down the street scarp of hill
still looking for the one
to whom one can feel grateful
in the cellar club the lift off
the jazz he finally gets
the jitter of jive
the steampunk skilful saxophone
be-bop-de-bop – scarred
dangerous men malarkey girls
the slicker money's grabbed
then down the drain
and while we're at it I think I'm allowed
one brutal cliché
the joyous monkey on the piano
wide split its wolf grin strikes
a misericord
the kind of bowel-moving moment where you want
to think backwards
how did we happen to this?
how did we come?
The retro chalice slips from the priest's grasp
spilling its contents onto the
congregation's collective face –
they don't seem to mind that they are now painted
with ineffable guiltless relaxation
full body contact rotating
out of the church door, steel-barred,
into the street
  – and the grinding business
of finding something not rotten to eat...

The End of Love

Let us acknowledge the ending of Love,
be grateful for what it teaches us.
Let us follow where it goes, the lenses
focussed where the hairs cross.

Let us celebrate its flight into penumbra,
That strict repeating click of metronome,
the swinging ellipse of pendulum
and wrecking ball, just before the turn,

that spot where compressed light begins to burn,
the maximum swell of waves
before collapse,
that place where once-immortal circles breach their arcs and
fracture to parallel lines, proclaiming, each one,
their fixed insularity forever...

And now let us watch for the single crystal
as it enters to command alone
that narrowest of passage points
where slips in time the glassed-in sand.

As captains and princes dying on our ships and bridges
and in palaces, where sweet poise rules
just before revolution's tempest: Let us stand and gaze.
It is so menacingly brief. Let us look out for
that pivotal ending of love, the extra inch
that breaks the tower, the gramme
that brings the camel down,
that mighty bit of groaning power, last and small,
that could tip the moon,
were she only to consent...

Or this ridged coin's edge where the flat world finishes
spinning, tossed for luck
and where tenacious as an ant I clamber
to the other surface
and discover a land leached of all precious element,
salted and black and pierced with a cross.
X.

As Winter Dies

I'm doubtful about these willows that lurch
and proliferate in the ice-melt of marsh.
And the catkins, dangling, so flippant and sly;
their choreographed attack amazingly
uncanny; that hazel bush tinged with green mist,
the hawthorn too, with its blight of shoots.
What is happening?

And there is more:
Those sinister crocuses inching up
and, with quiet, offensive charm, an assault of snowdrops.
There is something wrong with winter, its clean, iron grip.
It withers and rots with a verdant bloom on once-white cheeks.
It begins to die and a bird's celebratory cry
wins me over with havoc of song.

The Return of Her

She comes back trudging
over desert edges

thrusts her way through alleys
between broken buildings

her coat touching ground
a musky hint of verdant trail

on destroyed mortar delicate things
start to creep

the bomb-shelled birds stir to sound again singing
and scarred trees weeping with raw new sap

rising up she forces slabs and bricks
to accommodate such flowers as she chooses

the air softens and swells with charmed breezes
channelled from the south

she lumbers and slouches oblivious and indifferent
to this sick charnel house we have made

casts a cloak of worms over corpses
that once were frozen

she could take this whole fried city
– smashed roads burnt patches tumbled girders

no match for her sweeping surge of seeds her countless
nibbling mulching creatures – we too if we wish

could strip off armour and uniform
breathe in rich aromas of earth and green grass of

her skirt as she strides by welcoming and worshipping her
– Spring – Persephone – cleansing everything.

Spring Snow

A surprise of snowflakes, keeping military silence:
White soldiers, in their trillions, descend
from some big, invisible mother-cloud above.

They swirl and leap, uplifted by breezes,
touching each to each, creating even bigger flakes,
then ruthlessly attach to all points – curves, spikes and finules.

Nothing is immune: horses and bonnets
of children and buses, thin, looped wires,
the tender twigs of Spring, bent almost to snapping.

This gradual concert of invasion spreads down and on,
even to a robin's chicks, huddled naked in a box.
It creeps through keyholes, door cracks, chimneys, softening contours.

Briefly, on your eyelashes, some privileged crystals perch.
You call them melted angels as they form ersatz tears.
I watch from under your parasol – today, so misnamed –

and the flakes above betray their simple intent;
to make amorphous all else, with their intricate dead weight,
thrumming on the panels of taut blue silk.

Already It Has Risen

The sun has already risen.
It slashes merciless rays,
Spreading vitamin D and radiation equally.
The paint on the front door peels
under its ferocious examination.
It pours through the keyhole
easy as milk.

Nestling its shape quite solid on the floor,
its onslaught over, it marks a question;
its position and shape ever shifting slightly,
but laying the same question each cloudless day.
Then the cat pats the intangible spot
 – golden like butter – and jumps
as a tumble of letters land.

Happy Moment

One Happy Moment
is lurking in the corner,
next to the sofa.
It shifts to the desk
in the fluffy nest
of snaky cables.
Now it's moved to the sideboard
waiting to break out
of the bowl of nuts.

One Happy Moment
is suffocating
in a zipped cushion
and yet I hear it scratching
behind that picture
of a Dutch woman
ministering to her man
in a cool, tiled,
home of happiness.

One Happy Moment
is looking at me,
it's leapt to my knee;
leached of all colour,
so transparently clear.
Should I stroke it like a cat
or leave it untouched,
to freely float, unbesmirched,
into the happy garden?

I Have Always Yearned to See

... what cannot be seen –
The sumptuous sweat of oil garnered
in deep honeycombs below
the regal black of water lakes
glassy under desert sand
the bedrock sanctuary of lands
cached safe beneath the weight of seas
and the deliquescent magma base
molten at the middle of earth
compressed and forced to spin
it spins like a beaten sun.

And the cracks where the love streams in.

Dreaming a sleep without dreamers
all the colours beyond red and violet
the hidden side of moon
and the space between atoms
that hold together tight oceans and my room
and what split realm films continuous
here in my blind spot?
What deft exercise commands unvigilant
when angels and astronauts collide uncomprehending
actors in the mist behind my brow
here, where you are not?

I Have Yearned to Hear

... what cannot be heard:
Scream of hooked wet fish,
squeals of up-rooted tubers,

snowflakes colliding to land
on my single clapping hand
grasping a ruined telephone

whistling no news of abandoned pit canaries
gassed and blackened
in tuneless corridors far below

and then, the fragile wheeze, light as dust,
of the last-ever unicorn's final breath
spreading in a whisper of river mist

and what must the passing of the mute swan be like
as, unearthly, wings bent back, beak wide,
it summons its unique and perfect end?

What cry is flung, eldritch, from heart to sky,
sobbing its bud of hidden truth away,
unravelling, in début song of death?

Submerged Village

Nobody knows how exactly they live,
the folks who never left,
when their village was submerged
 – a sudden sea, a cliff-top cleft and stiffened ghosts in shock.
We may assume they carry on their businesses

in usual ways, affirming each to each that all's well,
though possibly the baker might suspect
his cobs are overly soft and salt,
and the dovetail joints of the carpenter
must surely vex him as they swell.

But when the Sunday bell peels out, I doubt it not,
the vicar's unresisting flock will slash a path through weed
to a damp church, battling fishes away like gnats,
admiring and judging late-laboured bonnets and skirts,
except for the village fool, dreaming of birds and stars.

The Place That Ever Is

I have been here before and will be again
like the tide that laps the salt marshes,
not trying to colonise,
but if walls and causeways surrender,
then let it be just so.

I walk by a village half submerged,
the clank of a muffled church bell disturbs;
hefty strides squelch on buried histories.
I imagine the last wagons leaving
with pots and pans a-rattle,

the mighty smith with anvil and irons
and proud name – he could end up anywhere –
in a mud field – a town would grow around him –
and we must trust that he chooses wisely to settle
a place not prone to flood nor pestilence

nor treacherous cliffs where, we all remember,
the pretty shepherdess entirely tumbled to her death.
So many strands to this unfinished tale!
The smith's son, who doted on her, practises his oar strokes.
He plans to retrieve the bell, claiming it for solace.

He will hang it on a scaffold in his own new yard
and grimly strike it for his pleasure and anguish
(its unjubilant message morbid reminder
of the un-jumped marriage fire)
or die trying there in the sea's embrace.

I have visited that place also,
I am tugged between the two
 – the water, the firm land – these times and those –
as waves of air, I am become a season, not a thing,
my breath scrolling metal stories to the wind.

Jigsaw

All the straight edges in place,
one long rambling briar of thorn,
pinned to the boundary wall with wire
and the obvious easy sides of thatch,
while the future blue, disjointed still, sits in a jumble.

On this idyll they work together.
So much empty space to fill,
on which they place cold cups of tea
as the difficult wind screams nonsense outside,
tearing late flowers, rattling the house.

I am a three thousand piece heavy-duty
commissioned jigsaw of their new-bought cottage dream.
He took the photograph on a cloudless morning,
not thinking of the fiendishness of clear lapis sky
nor the seed-packet collage of their riotous garden.

He concentrates on upright hollyhocks
 – these are the not too hard bits –
and the cinder path running west to east,
connecting him to her, right opposite and lost
in a thicket of exuberance – yellow, white and pink.

He never really wants to make me whole,
my pretty, comforting picture all done,
yet inserts the last piece with a flourish;
behind a diamond pane window, blurred face
ghostly image of a child.

This is the sixth time they have consummated me
to fill the dark October nights.
He always keeps the same last piece in his pocket
 – final fragment of the gone boy they never talk about.
He hammers it in and she pretends joy.

Bathtime

Stretching in a rare metal bath,
seeping old bones in a luxury of water,
feverish from a fit of flu:
I am told they used to make gin or kept the coal in
this Victorian trophy.

I view twin islands of my knees,
little atolls of my toes,
and a strange Sargasso weedy patch
where the bobbing penis floats,
a one-eyed Kraken.

It is all a swamp. Mists swirl. Tang of pine.
I wallow lazy like a buffalo,
pondering past victories, revived;
that sumptuous she-buffalo I rolled over once
long times ago. I grope for the lost soap.

Ducks and boats capsize,
whole continents sink,
creatures swimming for their lives
to the forest of my hair.
Atlantis surges as a limb.

Splish splash the bubbles swirl
and surplus skin collapses into scum.
I lean back on white enamel, breathing slow.
The topography of my body reassembles
in its confined narrow sea with all its aches.

The Scylla and Charybdis of my knees rest.
The Kraken sleeps.
Fresh settlements of refugees I plant on risen breast
and suffer them to live in peace, immune from drips,
my god-like drama spent.

This tub, they say, is haunted
by a suicide.
All her warm red dreams flowed pulsing...
A cold dead country, blue-lipped and dreamless,
waiting for someone else to find.

When We Woke Up

When we woke up we discovered ourselves
holding ridiculous emblems and sceptres
amid rods and bangles of authority,
of weaponry and religious badges
and some quite obvious accoutrements of slavery.

We were a mound of bodies
piled up next to neat-dug strips of trenches.
Wondering whether they were for our own burial,
or some war butchery we were supposed to take part in;
this exercised our minds but briefly,

for we had then to consider the apparel we wore;
an unmistakeable mix of brute uniform and shroud,
which we began to pull off and tear
in a fever of renunciation.
But then there was the matter

of the empty flagons and sickly drugs
still clotting sweet in peoples' mouths – evidence
obviously of forced feeding we all agreed.
Later, those with unexplained babies claimed rape.
Our keenest historians had already begun work.

Nobody told us where to go
so we built big gardens and houses right there,
using the old ironmongery to separate pigs
from the vegetables and we let memories slide,
for all had been embarrassed and we needed to forget.

Sometimes, though, I wonder;
Suspicion, it seems, is rising, regarding those others
on the other side of the hill, the river, the wire;
dark mutterings of disapproval; the way they walk,
the way they hold themselves, their different clothes.

Flood

I love it when the moon sucks us up like this
and our bodies swell with rain from a far country
and where we lie, filling ditches, rivers, drains, lakes;
we break our boundaries and barriers, spilling over, joining

our brothers, who dropped to land before us
and our wild sisters who coursed downwards,
ever downwards, coming from distant hills where they fell.
We rise, we rebels and we flow, go where we oughtn't.

Invaders of the dry flats. Of esplanades and tow paths.
Of roads and pavements. Gardens. Door steps.
And especially of cellars. Which we pack with our
wetness as we stuffed the sewers before them.

So much to explore in a mutual sniff of excitement
– these curious desiccant stores of the land; we lick potatoes,
roots of all kinds, leathers, wood; we love to find cottons,
woollens, jute, any porous stuff to soak and make a home in.

We explore ever upwards – we discover carpets.
Furniture, curtains, books. We creep our tendrils up,
up, penetrating under doors, floors, floral wallpaper...
The people, oh, the people – they pump, they wail, they evacuate.

I nestle nicely in a sandbag, turning it to cosy sludge,
watch the fishes play among the swim of floating chairs, dead dogs.
Here comes a car now, sailing, bobbing, a bubble of air,
trailing its oily sheen, rainbow patterns in its wake.

After the Catastrophe

After the catastrophe
the grim shake down
crying in the snow
breaking hail
rattle of rain
spoilt straw
end of law

the inevitable occupation:
Refugees in ruins
of castles, manors, bungalows.

First the food, then the clothes,
the furniture for fuel,
looting expeditions – no –
let us call it foraging:
For metal, tools, for pots,
for knives, cups, for picture books
and shampoo.

They wondered about the soaps and lotions
and shampoos. In tiled, white, useless bathrooms
grimed with the last of unflushed shite so many
bottles and tubes of salves and talcs and oils
and thick nourishing jellies.

Those who knew to read would entertain;
horse-chestnut, jojoba, ti tree, chamomile...
Several on the go – how rich they were –
those golden people of the cosmetic age,
with their never quite finished pastes and mascaras and dyes.

Here, behind a barricade of bricks and girders,
a brigade chief's daughter lovingly lathers
Sainsbury's own-brand washing-up liquid
into her wild, lemon-scented, pink hair.

When Time Stops

Who dares now shout in the mountains?
The last echoes swallowed in the solitude of canyons.
Unmoving is the scree and boulders are stilled.
In the valley sparks no longer fly from the old anvil,
it is wedged high in a cleft of oak
and twisted the plough lodges useless in roots of iris.
Rust marks streak where adamant iron stood.
The pages of the book are glued together shut.

Flutes are stopped with sand, harp strings cut.
There is no shelter but sky, lungs stifle on dust
yet the graves are filled with green coal only,
for time itself has struck! trembling to proceed,
like an overwhelmed clock-spring. It is afraid:
It has watched all the churches in the world en-flamed.
It has seen oceans, deserts, forests, trade places.
It has stretched beyond sense. The long game is up.

It demands surcease now and brakes and stops
in the middle of this robin's racing song, mouth open:
And leaps the pitchforked jab snatching a sob from my defeat,
twin tines pinning my wings down.
The roar of dinosaur has become bird squeak
then silence as I testify and witness
and in this collapsed instance all things unfurl themselves
revealed beyond all the ages and awake.

The Future

This is what the future feels like:
Air holds just a touch of metal
though each day drops like an anvil
voiding experience of storm-blitzed night
bulldozing compressed dreams away.
Together at dawn talented birds squeeze
firm hard beaks into tight little songs
like cherry diamonds in crisp ether.
Leaves shiver and thrash on trees
rash chickens run loose
cows bury their own green pancakes.
Evolution has lurched far beyond italics
stumbling over the present
the tense wait is over a different sun commands.
The fool knowing his place at cliff edges
scotching his loop trying to bite the moon
gathering wanton stars to his own rope bed.
Each corner has its feisty collection
of swept shadows the lean spider smells
huddled grandmothers in shreds
bidding in remembrance to smears on the pavement
faces devoured by the wrong rain
sorting and creaming with milk pale grimy babies
and where lodged once the windows
yet still flicker constant streaks of light unstable
all is loose in the stitch much is rubbed out
as though by uncontrollable maids
whose confused living attics resounding sing
and some hieroglyphs survive the mess unscarred
in glassy sand fast-tracked stamped and printed to fossil.
For this is a language used still to alleviate
the permanent trailing burn of love
by monsters of ceremonies injecting tears
and always he who keeps the standard
bar outstanding silver from the mud
conducting music of flowers lives on
in our blood with strings of D.N.A. untramelled
the chemical trader is sudden king
and with shock of feelings coming back in
write it in charcoal everlasting:
Only the just endure only the just.
Now at last let bent nails get revenge on the hammers
let us at least not spend the final night
munching our own canaries in the dark.

The End

This is it, the end.
What end? The end of a piece of rope;
the short end, the thin end, the whipping end.

The end of story, end of a line, of lives
bravely boring through tunnels and cellars,
abandoning prisons and citadels,

to end in a horrible meadow of pleasure.
Too many aristos. A sewerage of aristos.
Their statues consume the realm.

Blight takes the vineyards,
starved roots clamber coffins
filled with murdered thoughts.

This is the end of a very long note
that curves in a plume like a doomed aeroplane
to crash in a perfect chord:

Smashed ivory splinters. The final rhino.
The last of the sandal trees – and the cedar.
This is the end of the desert – the sea:

Nowhere else to go. Film finished.
Book closed. Lap-top lid shut.
Radio knob turned left till the click and the fading glow

of irreplaceable valves,
their burnt dust smell
and only future archaeologists to guess and to tell

what use keyboards and guns, bath-taps and telephones,
the thin, un-maternal shape of Barbie Doll statuettes
and ice-cream scoops.

The end of ice:
All melted then; the last of it licked
by trolls on the summits,

cactus sidling up the slopes,
the end of tumbling primroses then.
The end of Spring. This is the end, my friend.

Inheritance

They came with their breathing apparatus
and caterpillar tracks
slouching over rubble.

Please do not crush our gardens, we begged.
They said, why are the trees so bleak
and the flowers shrunk back into ground,

why do rivers foam with creamy silt
and flooded shorelines reek of death.
Where has all the blue gone

and the feathered things, are they, too, gone?
And we replied, we do not know this blue you seek,
is it a weed? Tell us what you need:

We fashion blankets out of plastic
and make insect cakes to eat
and we drink warm glowing water from the well.

This is what we hold, this earth,
we call it our inheritance.
You are welcome. We are the meek.

Time To Leave

It is time to leave and the door is open.
I am prepared as a waxed silk thread pulled,
stiffly enters the needle's eye.

It was good, the bread and wine, the house;
the wooden bed, the metal pail, stone hearth,
the travail and repose, the old violin.

But everything was always borrowed, even the cups
and, like the sculpted animals in a plaything ark,
it is time to put them away.

But I would keep you, my love,
my words are not enough
and never finished.

This, the never-ending chime of my last goodbye,
contains a thousand syllables,
disappearing through a gap in the clouds.